Dear Darlene

You are in our prayers

With love
Pauline Bitonti
Carol Vought.
Sylvia Miller

Published by Barbour Books, an imprint of Barbour Publishing, Inc., P.O. Box 719, Uhrichsville, Ohio 44683, www.barbourbooks.com

Member of the
Evangelical Christian
Publishers Association

Printed in China.
5 4 3 2 1

Our Prayers Are with You

ELLYN SANNA

At the start of each new day,

take courage from this knowledge:

We are praying for you.

More things are wrought by prayer
than this world dreams of.

ALFRED, LORD TENNYSON

You are in our prayers.

We ask for. . .
God's Love All Around You
God's Peace in Your Heart
God's Wisdom to Guide You
God's Gentleness to Dry All Your Tears
God's Strength for Each Day

We constantly pray for you,
that our God may count you worthy of his calling,
and that by his power he may fulfill
every good purpose of yours
and every act prompted by your faith.

2 THESSALONIANS 1:11

I

God's Love
All Around You

The light of God surrounds me;
The love of God enfolds me;
The power of God protects me;
The presence of God watches over me.
Wherever I am, God is.

JAMES DILLET FREEMAN

Wherever I go—only Thou!
Wherever I stand—only Thou!
Just Thou, again Thou, always Thou!
When things are good—Thou!
When things are bad—Thou!
Thou, Thou, Thou!

JEWISH PRAYER

There is not a step you take,
not a word you speak,
not a moment of your entire life,
when you are not surrounded by the love of God.
But busyness, stress, worries, and even life's pleasures
so easily blind our eyes to God's presence.
We pray today that you may have grace to know
you are totally wrapped in God's love.
His love is all around you.
Like a newborn held close in its mother's arms,
you are completely safe.

Keep me as the apple of your eye;
hide me in the shadow of your wings.

PSALM 17:8

You are the apple of God's eye.
He delights in you.
Like a loving mother who watches her child
with tenderness, care, and joy,
God is watching over you,
loving you,
keeping you,
and enjoying your presence.

Christ with me, Christ before me, Christ behind me,
Christ in me, Christ beneath me, Christ above me,
Christ on my right, Christ on my left,
Christ when I lie down, Christ when I sit down,
Christ when I arise,
Christ in the heart of everyone that thinks of me,
Christ in the mouth of everyone who speaks of me,
Christ in every eye that sees me,
Christ in every ear that hears me.

PRAYER OF ST. PATRICK

We pray today that
you may sense the presence of Christ
in each place you go,
in each person you meet,
in each action you take,
and in every breath you breathe.

II

God's Peace
in Your Heart

I was overcome by trouble and sorrow.
Then I called on the name of the Lord:
"O Lord, save me!"...
Our God is full of compassion.
The Lord protects the simplehearted;
when I was in great need, he saved me.
Be at rest once more, O my soul,
for the Lord has been good to you.
For you, O Lord, have delivered my soul from death,
my eyes from tears,
my feet from stumbling.

PSALM 116:3–8

We pray that your heart may be "simple" enough
to know that God is with you.
We all tend to make things so complicated;
we worry and fret over the details—
when God is quietly asking us
to surrender them all into His hands.
Like Mary of Bethany,
we need to be mindful of just one thing:
the presence of Christ in our lives.
When you are overcome with troubles,
He will give you rest.
You can depend on Him.
His love never fails.
Trust Him and be at peace.

Father, I abandon myself into Your hands.
Do with me whatever You will.
Whatever You may do, I thank You.
I am ready for all, I accept all.
Let only Your will be done in me,
And in all Your creatures.
Into Your hands I commend my spirit.
I offer it to You with all the love that is in my heart.
For I love You, Lord, and so want to give myself,
To surrender myself into Your hands,
Without reserve and with boundless confidence,
For You are my Father.

CHARLES DE FOURCAULD

Let nothing disturb thee,
Nothing affright thee:
All things are passing;
God never changeth;
Patient endurance
Attaineth all things;
Who God possesseth
In nothing is wanting;
Alone God sufficeth.

TERESA OF AVILA

Why should I feel discouraged?
Why should the shadows fall?
Why should my heart feel lonely
And long for heaven and home?
When Jesus is my portion.
A constant friend is He.

I sing because I'm happy,
I sing because I'm free.
His eye is on the sparrow,
And I know He watches me.

AFRICAN-AMERICAN SPIRITUAL

When I was a little girl, I used to sing this spiritual over and over: "I sing because I's happy, I's sing because I's free," my mother says I would sing as I played. I still remember the feeling of safety and joy those words gave me. I was free to sing because Jesus was keeping track of me. I was just a little girl—but if He cared about small brown birds, then I was convinced He would watch over me as well. When my heart was troubled, those words brought peace.

Thou, from whom to be turned is to fall,
to whom to be turned is to rise,
and in whom to stand is to abide forever;
grant us in all our duties Thy help,
in all our perplexities Thy guidance,
in all our dangers Thy protection,
and in all our sorrows Thy peace;
through Jesus Christ our Lord.

SAINT AUGUSTINE

Our peace is so easily disturbed.
   The nightly news. . .
      paying the bills. . .
         our worries about loved ones. . .
            a visit to the doctor. . .
               work responsibilities. . .

Any and all of these can upset our interior sense of quiet and well-being. We almost feel *obliged* to spend our lives feeling uneasy and on edge; peace seems like a luxury we can't afford.

But peace is a divine gift that is ours for the taking.
   As children of God, it is our heritage.
      May you reach out and take this precious gift.
         Don't be afraid.
            God wants you to have it.

The LORD bless thee, and keep thee:
The LORD make his face shine upon thee,
and be gracious unto thee:
The LORD lift up his countenance upon thee,
and give thee peace.

NUMBERS 6:24–26 KJV

III

God's Wisdom to Guide You

May you have hope
to look forward to happy tomorrows.
May you have courage to face life's hardships
and faith to follow Christ even when the way is dark.
May your joy in Him lead you to serve others.
I ask that He will show you the gifts He has given you,
so that you may put them to good use,
daring to make a difference in our world.
May you be wise enough to know
both your limitations and your strengths.
May you always follow Jesus.

The Lord is my shepherd, I shall not be in want.

He makes me lie down in green pastures,

he leads me beside quiet waters,

he restores my soul.

He guides me in paths of righteousness

for his name's sake.

PSALM 23:1–3

O Lord, this is our desire—to walk along the path of life that You have appointed us, in steadfastness of faith, in lowliness of heart, in gentleness of love. Let not the cares or duties of this life press on us too heavily; but lighten our burdens, that we may follow Your way of quietness, filled with thankfulness for Your mercy; through Jesus Christ our Lord.

Maria Hare

Lead us, O Father, in the paths of peace,
Without Your guiding hand we go astray,
And doubts appall and sorrows still increase;
Lead us through Christ, the true and living Way.

WILLIAM BURLEIGH

Let us make our way together, Lord:

wherever You go

I must go:

and through whatever You pass,

there too I will pass.

TERESA OF AVILA

When you are confused,
when you cannot see the road ahead,
when right seems like wrong and wrong like right,
when your head aches trying to
sort through the demands placed upon you,
we pray that in that moment
you will turn to God.
Wait on Him.
His wisdom will show you the right way to go.

IV

God's Gentleness to Dry All Your Tears

The Golden Hour

Jim Rohn says, "Invest the first hour of the day, the 'Golden Hour,' in yourself." How much richer will be your investment when you spend that hour alone with God! Tell Him your concerns and pain. Sit in silence, waiting for His gentle hand to touch your heart. Allow Him to soothe the pain that troubles you. Soak up His tender mercies. This time alone with God is truly more precious than gold.

Prayer is the key of the morning

and the bolt of the evening.

MATTHEW HENRY

Come to me,

all you who are weary and burdened,

and I will give you rest. . .

.for I am gentle and humble in heart,

and you will find rest for your souls.

MATTHEW 11:28–29

Have you ever been asked to drop backward into someone's waiting arms? It's an exercise in trust. Not being able to see, confident only in the other person's ability—and willingness—to catch you, you have to let yourself fall. It's not an easy thing to do. *What if they don't catch me?* our minds whisper. Unable to relax and fall limply backward, we put a foot back, catch ourselves, refuse to simply trust.

God asks us to drop into His arms. We claim to have faith—and yet when it comes down to it, we tense up; we catch ourselves before we even quite fall.

We don't need to be afraid to trust Him, though. When our hearts are hurting, His love and mercy is waiting to catch us. He is strong enough for the heaviest sorrow—and He will never let us drop.

All we have to do is trust—and fall into His arms.

$\mathcal{D}o$ not be afraid to throw yourself on the Lord!
He will not draw back and let you fall!
Put your worries aside and throw yourself on Him;
He will welcome and heal you.

SAINT AUGUSTINE

The eternal God is your refuge,

and underneath are the everlasting arms.

DEUTERONOMY 33:27

The LORD preserveth the simple:
I was brought low, and he helped me.

PSALM 116:6 KJV

Rely on God when your heart is heavy.
He can comfort the deepest pain.
His love is gentle,
and His mercy is great.

V

God's Strength
for Each Day

How can you find the strength you need?
Through prayer.
How can you pray?
By simply centering your heart on God.
Pay attention to what He is doing in your life.

It is prayer that

restores to us the ability to feel,

to see, and to appreciate.

REUBEN HAMMER

Jesus said, "Watch and pray."
This is what we are doing in centering prayer.
Watching is just enough activity to stay alert.
Praying is opening to God.

THOMAS KEATING

*I don't know how to pray,
but I know how to pay attention.*

MARY OLIVER

Prayer turns even our heaviest burdens
into blessings. . .
and gives us strength.

We learn to walk by stumbling.

BULGARIAN PROVERB

Don't be afraid to stumble.
Watch a toddler learning to walk;
when he falls, he simply picks himself up
and tries again.
Sometimes he cries a little at first—
and you may too when you stumble over life's rough spots—
but your heavenly Father is waiting to dry your tears,
set you on your feet again,
and help you learn to walk.
He is not disappointed in you.
He only wants to help you find the strength you need
to continue on your way,
until one day, you won't be walking anymore. . .
you'll be flying!

God, please, we ask You,

to help our loved one rely on You.

Help her to find new strength in You.

May she take courage from Your Spirit.

Restore the heart, inspire the mind,

and renew the body,

we pray

for Your name's sake.

Amen.

As each day draws to a close
and you settle down to sleep,
please know:
You have been in our thoughts throughout the day,
and now, as we too end our day,
we offer you up once more to God.
And when tomorrow comes,
our prayers will continue to be with you.

I lie down and sleep;
I wake again,
because the Lord sustains me.

PSALM 3:5